Farewell, Samsara

For dear Tom,
who keeps beautifying
my garden and
enriching my life
with friendship —
Love,
Margaret
10-5-2013

Farewell, Samsara

Selected Poems
by
Margaret Henderson Hager

Philadelphia

doctormhager@gmail.com

Farewell, Samsara
First Edition, Paperback - published 2013

ISBN: 978-0-9896511-0-3

House Call is reprinted with permission of the Philadelphia County
Medical Society. It appeared in Volume 86, Number 1 (January 1990) of
Philadelphia Medicine.

Printed in the United States of America

To my dearest parents, Frances and Bobby,
who nurtured my sensitivity, encouraged my writing,
supported my pursuit of medicine,
and whose love will always be with me.

Contents

House Call

When will the time be right to sum up,
To finally record her case, called to the bedside
To still the wheeze,
To ease the tightness in her chest,
Asked to stretch into weeks the days left,
To transfuse the sand steadily slipping
Through the neck of a fragile hourglass,
Then with success, to see the spirit reemerge,
Whose laughter once rippled through the curtains
Of these windows before
They closed down upon a sickroom.
On good days she greets with obliging smile
From the prison of her couch,
Its table strewn with tubes and vials,
Schedules to keep the balance and sustain,
The hissing green metal tank at her feet,
A warning serpent.

Instead of ripening summer brings decline.
No more reprieves. All that remains
In the black bag, an anodyne, to comfort only.
There is a pact not to rescue if she slips.
Now, I return with little to offer.
To chart the fever, check the weak pulse,
Bend close for whispers from her lips,
To watch the fall and rise of her frail chest,
Silence followed by heaving breath, then
When it seems forever, suddenly, it ceases.
There is nothing more but to close her eyes in death,
Discreetly shut the door,
Put away the instruments into the leather bag,
Sign the forms, file the chart,

Now just pages in a record kept for a set span
Of time.

How well I know in my heart,
All that could be done is done. Though the time is right,
So often before this task performed, I hesitate to close.
What stops me now? Looking down at her lifeless form
I recall another final embrace, not yet a year
Past. I see another face: Father!
The door is open to a flood of tears.

Gathering Chestnuts

A sudden scent penetrates the chill air,
The sound of crackling, rusted leaves underfoot:
A scene lit by slanting, long afternoon rays
Carries me back on the swell of years.
I see her: wispy blonde, brown-eyed,
Standing in a shaft of light,
Wearing a little plaid coat of red and green,
Nearby a willow-basket rolling full,
Of horse-chestnuts, the crop of small fat hands.
Gazing down with eyes of blue-crystal,
A woman's face, framed in fine white hair.
Bending over her, a dark-haired man of thirty,
Who stoops to brush away the leaves,
Then turns, for her to discover alone
Yet another mahogany jewel,
One more trophy of Fall,
Seized gleefully, then tossed into the till.
Their eyes meet in unquestioning trust.

Suddenly returned to now by a chill gust,
I wonder how long I have been sitting here lost,
On this gray wooden bench in the rose-garden,
Afternoon now blended into dusk:
A still from so long ago, brought back
By the scent of moldering leaves,
The sight of brown stands of trees against
This deep blue sky.
So long ago now yet still clear,
A memory sealed in this time capsule,
A smooth brown chestnut, clutched
Forty years later in my hands.

Eunate

For John S.

It rises starkly from a naked plain,
Ringed at the limn by Pyrenees,
This octagon of sandstone, weather-worn,
Shining in the sun, as clouds now part
Like curtains to unveil a backlit stage:
This temple tempered by eight hundred years
Of scorching sun and icy winds at turns,
The origin and meaning of its name, obscure,
As nomads settled here to then move on.
Moors, then Christians following in time,
Leaving behind in enigmatic layers
Ways and words amidst the broken shards:
Eunate, in itself a prayer.

Here something hallowed hangs in arid air,
Where twisting sandstone columns point toward sky.
Deep in the sanctum, ancient bones repose,
Both saints and sinners, buried in this ground,
All called one time to make this pilgrimage
Onward to Compostela on the coast,
The shrine of Santiago of the shells.
Through dry and dusty plains they trod the road,
Scourged on their way by gales or gripping heat,
The mountains undulating in the haze.
What welcome sight, this chapel in a field,
Shelter from snow, yet cool in summer's rage:
Eunate, sacred sundial of the soul.

And you and I repeat this journey now,
Cross half a globe to follow in these steps.

Upon our harried lives a hush descends
The feeling deepens, as our ears perceive
Voices echoing within the chapel walls,
Beckoning across the bare autumnal plain,
Which sandstone blocks now starkly demarcate,
Bear witness to the spirit's ceaseless search,
This mystic place, once thronged with seekers,
Drawn here by will and fear in equal parts,
Entraps us in the warp's forgotten years,
This temple stranded in the sands of time,
As Eunate pulls us through a door.

Caught in the woven tapestry of days,
Now tangible, a yearning human presence,
A sense of fear and hope, and hardship borne,
All to buy the soul a berth in heaven,
The price exacted of their weary faithful feet,
The cobbled village square left far behind,
Casting their lot as pilgrims, to the road,
Plodding beyond a small horizoned world
Through rugged mountain pass and rock-strewn way,
To reach that healing shrine upon the coast.
Yet, at this gateway to refresh and rest,
At Eunate, wellspring of the faith.

A mournful chorus lifts and fills the air:
"Santa Maria!" women cry for grace,
A ray of hope to touch this brutish life,
Or just the promise of a gentle death
And roadmap to the perfect world beyond.
The chant drones on with tambourine and drum,
Conjures dark-eyed men and women's faces.
Reflecting fear of hell and heaven's bliss,

Their lives play out a brief but hectic dance,
Whose churning wake vibrates in traces,
Now washes over us in surging waves.
On this bleak plain within these sandstone walls,
We stand transfixed in Eunate's timeless trance.

September

Fields of goldenrod fly past, blurs
Of yellow and brown, gradually replacing green,
Through traffic and commotion
As we careen across this highway
There is a sense of life's motion.
Amber in the sun's rays, now oblique,
Corn shocks cover fallow farmland.
There is the chill scent of crimson days
That lie ahead: leaves will turn yellow,
Brown, then fall dry to the ground.
A dying monarch floats slowly down
On the damp breeze: the cicadas' chorus slows,
Then all at once goes mute: nowhere,
To be found, a magic, life-prolonging potion,
The cycle is completing, and too acutely,
I feel the motion.

Grounding

Thoughts of earlier years
When dreams carried us
Far from the task at hand,
From the book, the microscope,
From paper and pen,
When it was far more tempting
To look outward
To the wider view without boundary,
An open window of hope,
Beyond the familiar farmland,
Where in hills sweet with clover
Surrounded by furrowed fields
We reached consciousness.
Then, there was the need to leave,
Follow the burning dream,
Write words that would blaze
As torches to eternity,
Hold the passion and the belief fast
That one and only one truth
And, in fact, this one could last.

But now, time, relentless humbler,
Reveals, in life's middle years, that
The opposite is true: not the great vision,
Instead, the tool has become the center,
Our work, the glue and solid framework
To hold together fragile pieces.

Not the boundless, our comfort,
Instead, delineated space
And mundane habit are unveiled
As our grounding and the saving grace.

The River Fecht, Alsace

I awaken and know I have returned,
Hear for the first time, yet seem to recall,
The tolling of village bells at midnight,
The peal of chimes over orange-tiled roofs;
The wind waving yellow fields of rapeseed,
On an Alsatian summer morning.
Names call out from the distant past
As we move from grave to grave
In the well-tended churchyard,
The valley stretching out beneath,
Green hills thick with grapevine,
Below, the river Fecht flowing,
Constant in its flux,
Breathing stillness and peace
In contrast to the eddies of my soul.
This brook which felt the pounding
Of great-grandmothers' linens
On its cold, white stones,
Now reflects my face in middle-age,
Will see my granddaughters grow old.
Found, now, the deep source,
And during the rush of hours to come,
Far from this place, I will dip back
Into the water and remembering,
Be renewed.

Persephone Revisited

On, past hills and meadows of sepia tones,
She travels on this January day.
The red-tails, wings outstretched above
Point out the way along this country road.
The fields now turned to mud and mottled straw,
And woods like bundled twigs reach skyward
Where thin clouds hang suspended in gray-blue.

Not long ago, she dreaded winter's scene,
The brevity of day and length of night,
Sought avidly the warming southern rays,
Yearned for, craved, the waning light.
Now, looking out upon the naked world,
All unadorned by bud or flaming leaf,
Lacking rapture of Spring, and fire of Fall
She senses kinship in the early fading light
And comfort in the gray of sifting rain
No longer fears when roaring winds start
To shake the silver maple on her lane.
For now, they echo back her grieving heart
And in their moan, they resonate her pain.

Watching the Dawn Break
Quisisana, August 1992

Lake Kezar's waves have slapped the rocky point
Through the long night, fueled by winds
Which unrelenting, pour from northern skies,
Transform this lake to surf and fill our dreams
With ancient rhythms. Then from the southern edge
The orphic cry of a stirring loon
Whistles in primal echo over the cool,
The dark expanse, to then fall still.

Now first light, a misty curtain lifts,
Pale fire turns the far ridge yellow.
Over where old White Mountains sprawl
The shore's outline appears, pines and birch,
The slate-blue pond, whose rippling pleats
Crash, pounding the sand and pebble beach.

What outcome might this churning lake foretell?
What changes presaged by its roiling surge?
Above a cold sky hangs, its light-blue dome,
Serene, with wispy scattered clouds
Which cap, cling to the rounded mountain tops.

But waving firs bear only silent witness.
As I drink in this morning, fresh and pure,
My prayer goes out upon the lifting breeze:
That pristine shores like these will long endure
And dawns as wild as this one, never cease.

Casting My Line

I cast my line into the grey-blue water of the lake
In hope of catching those few magic words
To touch and move you from that distance,
Words to soothe you into trusting and believing.

Time elapses, sun past midday now,
But still no tug, only the wake
Of waves when the wind rustles through,
Willfully tossing scrub and birches
On the sandy edge of the lake.

And, so, I let out slack, add a weight
Row to the water's deepest spot
But still there's just the slightest pull.
A family of young mallards glides by,
Water lilies open and, in hours, close,
As the sun begins to dip, now the pond
Mirrors back golden brown.

I feel the line resist and reel it in,
The sad result is just a tangle,
The drag of thoughts caught weed-like,
On the hook, randomly snagged.

Now images of hearth, being together
Crowd in to taunt my solitude.
As evening air stirs on the water,
Picks up a chill, I come to wonder
If words or time or infinite patience
Will ever be rewarded, or if, instead,
In the dead of night, speechless, I'll pull in
An empty line, and alone head homeward.

Faith

Early morning, and the lake deep in mist.
Last evening, in sunset orange
The far shore lay studded in pines,
Here and there a beach cove
Or quiet cottage with wooden dock,
A few buoys bobbing on the ripples.
And later, as night progressed,
Deep contentment smiled from the face
Of a full, yellow moon
Reflected in peaty water.

Morning now, the mist thick, obscuring,
Blowing in wisps at the lake's edges,
And though the outline is indistinct,
Would I ever doubt that the ground
Still stands firm, as before,
Or that the firs and pines still wave,
Though out of sight, on the opposite shore?
Why should I not then believe,
Despite months of silence endured,
That what passed between us
A year ago or more still breathes?

The Mandrake

In supernatural night when the sky is blackest,
You are uncovered from this earthen bed,
Loose ground falling from your fleshy root,
By the bare crescent of waxing moon
An innocent plant pulled forth from darkness
And oblivion to develop magic might.

In the sacred hour, before birdsong,
The ancient incantation is intoned:
To be harnessed in focused passion
Carved with ritual blade
Then sealed in my blood, named
With that name dearer than my own
To be given back to earth in this hallowed glade
For one moon's time there
To become as his flesh and bone.

Return to earth now, Mandrake,
No longer free, now to do my bidding,
Become the magic link two souls inextricably
To bind: mute, insapient flower,
Complete the circle with the Cosmic mind,
That when I hold you in my palm
Under the next new moon, dried and stabbed
With silver pin, the charmed bond will be forged,
By smoking flame, the pentagram within,
And enchantment's spell cast. At last.

August, Lake Sunapee

Looking through the waving weeds
Wild mustard, fine brown grasses
Gone early to seed,
Bending in a morning breeze at nine
On the edge of the lake,
The sun creating diamonds
Refracting on the far rim,
The lake's stillness broken
By a lone canoe gliding
Through slate-blue water,
The high wind rattling tops of birches
Like crepe paper in a July parade,
For all the summers which life
Lends me to savor or to waste,
Out there lies an unchanging view,
Sky, water, the pines.
Eternity rises in a wet, blue gown,
Pulls me to her lips
Then slips back into the mirror of the lake.

Songs of Alberta
October 1991

Calgary to Banff

The plains roll on ahead, autumn well past,
Rusting hay bales rest in dormant fields,
And horses, manes grown heavy with the brush
Of first snowfall, and cattle, graze in peace,
Their faith vested in the Chinook's warm wind,
Fearless of the winter's fast approach.
At once they yield to herds of restless elk,
Who forage wild in the scrub of foothills,
Uneasy, less secure, their horoscope
Forged in the steel of ice-bound days ahead.

Then, suddenly, brown earth shifts to steel-gray rock,
Revealed, white peaks thrusting toward clouds,
And we lean back to crane, to catch the spires
Which disappear in mist to kiss the sky:
Confronted by this splendor, stark, sublime,
Our state of consciousness begins to change
As vast perspective dwarfs our lives and time.

Lake Louise

Beyond endless stretching, fallow plains
Where cloudless sky meets earth, in blue surround,
And dry winds rise to eat the early snow,
Where pines and birch accede to timberline,
She hears his voice command
This odyssey, this pilgrimage
To find a link, elusive grail,
This silent bond of understanding.

Unfolding now to disbelieving eyes:
This celebration, nature's highest Mass,
As prairie flows then folds to rugged hills,
Eliding upward into peaks of jagged rock,
Cathedrals forged of ice, incessant snow.
The train ascends through clouds, without a break,
Attains the crest, the valley down below.
Now breathless, from the heights, we view the lake.

Welling from its ancient glacial source,
The emerald princess of the Rockies glows:
Twin granite mountains plunge toward her,
Rival lovers, vying for her kiss,
Dipping hopeful into chill green water
Lapping upon the large smooth stones
Lining the edge, polished by grinding ice,
Mount Victoria reflected in this mirror,
Below lies Lake Louise, the royal daughter.
Raw evening air, blows waves of variscite,
Its murmur made of cumulative sighs
Released in awe at this glimpse,
As eyes, unready for sudden splendor,
Behold it now a liquid jewel,

Set in the crown of this rough, rocky range:
This is the sight he could not grasp in words,
Sent her these many miles to view alone—
How hard, to apprehend this pale green lake
Reminder of the heartbreak in his eyes.
In disbelief, hers close in meditation,
Stifling tears that rise and brim within:
Only to be free of passion's fierce ache!

As if in answer, a breeze lifts off the water
And stirs within a flooding recognition:
No cruel reproach, instead a gift, this sight,
In lieu of being his, a common ground:
To both have seen and loved this place.
Her open eyes drink in the water's hues:
Much more, to share in spirit than in flesh.
Now, peace descends, and with it comes reunion,
Transcending intervening time and space.
Instead of Lake Louise, his face stares back
Their beings join in this complete communion.

The Magic Mountain

Atop the cusp of Rundle's mount he climbs,
Eight thousand feet above his ocean origin,
A human form clings to the flat, stone face,
Scrambling to attain the pinnacle,
The goal, to gaze down from the world's roof
At all creation, stake dominion
For posterity, defy some ultimatum,
Attempt to numb his existential pain
With anesthesia of this alpine air,
Or exclude from his yearning spirit,
Those mundane fellow beings,
And elevate his striving, earthbound self
Through utter, elemental solitude.

The Mountain Village

Here, rests an inner sense of quiet joy,
Discovery of calm in pine-clad peaks,
The sought-for prototypic nest,
Lodged within the deep collective mind
A natural fortress, sanctuary,
Its air so much purer, being rare.
Below a river rushes from its glacial source
Then empties in an emerald lake. My view:
Two foreground pines, upright and thin,
Above, the Rundle jutting, white and grey
Into clouds, whose veiled wisps drift,
Its rock denying any human claim.
Up and up, it climbs in dizzy dance,
Imprints this scene upon a mind's slow film
Which until now knew only rolling hills,
The tumbling sea, surging in vast expanse,
Yet never dreamt of this extravagance.

Epilogue

The eye observes this scene in black and white,
In stark relief, then as sun breaks through,
And pines glow green, the sky a cobalt blue,
The lake, now emerald, after monochrome.
Here in this ancient habitat of peace:
The valley ringed by mountains' peaks,
Reminds us of a greater scale of time,
That underlies the briefness of our span,
Ephemeral our music, art and words,
All of brief estate in contrast to
The rising, then eroding force,
By wind and ice, of raging mountaintops.
They stood before, will long persist
When fragile flesh has melted back to loam,
After the memory of our race, each poem lost,
And every canvas, they will outlast,
The life we know, rocks covered in snow,
Standing to inherit all, when we must go.

Supplication to Spring

Speak for me, lilacs in shades deep purple to white,
Let your fragrance swell on May's soft wind,
Float out on the warm night air, intoxicate,
Weave the timeless spell well
Before summer breaks and it is too late.
Weeping cherry, pink stars still tight
Paper bark black in streaming rain
Absorb my image now,
So that when he gazes, awestruck
At the sight of your pastel cloud,
You will reflect my smile,
And he will recall, feel bittersweet pain.
Chorus of morning birds singing
Full-throat, exuberant
On the chill breeze at five,
Fill his sleeping mind
With dreams of Eden, revive
That heart which once beat harder, for my sake.
Speak for me, tender May,
Touch him with soft flower
And green velvet leaf:
It is the least you can do
And well within your power
For I have gone mute with his loss,
And all your blossoming just magnifies my grief.

Nocturne

The full moon stares down cool and white
Upon a leaf-strewn landscape
Mouth agape, in wistful disbelief
At the sight: fall, vermillion and gold
Yesterday, now decaying,
Fading like an aging photograph,
Life's brilliant pigments blanching
At winter's white edge.

But August's sun blazed hot a day ago,
Can winter's chill arrive so suddenly,
Evening swift upon the heels of noon,
So much left still to create, undone,
And all of this passed by so soon?

In that instant you recoiled, too late
From that blind, impulsive kiss
And locked my eyes with yours,
At once conscious of our fate,
Your gaze was like this autumn moon's.

Nocturne II

Some nights, Chopin, I have to wonder
If you aggravate or soothe love's pangs.
Your nocturnes swell, the piano sighs
You knew the torment all too well
And codified it in these chords.
But there is no intimation
In the haunting notes
If your private hell did ever end
Or if a balm existed which might heal
The wound which would not close,
If you found some way to palliate
That which we chose, you and I,
A storm-tossed fate instead of peace.

But you died young, disease's flush,
Not that of health on your cheeks,
The hectic red not passion's heat.
While we live on. Yet in this music
You survive, that glowing candle
Burning on through darkness,
Reminding with each dark crescendo,
As our lives are wrenched apart
His from mine, to try to reach beyond
The sense of wronging, find courage to accept,
Despite the hurt of loss and endless longing.

Fear of May

I fear the anniversary of that night
When the gentle May rain fell.
The memory of his sight,
Brash in plaid shirt and jeans
Leaning in my doorway
The cool breeze tossing wavy hair,
The air then suddenly clear
Revealing a full bright moon.
He stands on the threshold,
Unconscious of the tryst, yet undeclared
Until desire unleashed opens hungry arms
To catch and pull us back to fatal kiss
And the earth's motion is suspended.

Then all at once the full and yellow moon
Which just emerged,withdraws behind thick clouds.
And thunder's clash signals the magic's end:
At once arms release, he stands to go,
Never to return this way again.
And so I fear May's soft beginning,
And through its rainy nights I hear
The echo of love's unexpected arrival,
Dropping in like a rush of warm Spring air,
May's shower transformed to storm's derision,
And by the self-same breeze, I grieve,
Relive the stinging shock of pain,
In that swift immutable decision.
That though you loved, you had to leave.

One for the Road

Two years ago and more I knew
The day would come when
Buckling under the load,
I would set this burden down,
Lift the cup of despair
Once more to trembling lips
And drink to the lonely road. Long
Having watched this bitter fermentation,
Crying out from desperate dreams
To halt the vintage ripening:
Guilt, the vessel that contained it,
Fear, then finally pity, the cork.
Now decanted, this libation.
As it had to be, poured into the crystal
Of bitter resignation,
I grasp the goblet, drink to liberation
Having reached the exit-booth
At the end of hope's highway
And sadly paid the toll.

Comet

From nowhere, streaking through black space,
A comet approaches on a plotted course,
Until, drawn into orbit,
It comes close, rounding the earth
In magnetic embrace,
Held by gravity
It would seem forever,
But then, completing the turn,
It swings out parabolic
Into that endless ether,
Hurtling forth.
Now, in the empty sky
Just a comet's tail glowing
And I am left below to try to grasp
This coming
And going.

Record in Sand

Scottsdale, 1989

Sonoran winds breathe hot and dry,
As still and silent as death red hills lie —
This backdrop of cactus, desert scrub,
And time, a leather strap, tied wet
Across her naked breast, left to dry,
To cut, razor sharp into bare flesh,
Fanned by Arizona's parching air.

Now aware of what will come to pass,
She feels the resonating fear
As playing and replaying in her mind
The scene unfolds then closes unresolved.
Embrace, the searching kiss, to draw apart
His face amazed, the spell then shattered
As reason dawns, tearing him from the ledge,
To leave her clutching the rock face, bereft.

Now two lone figures, silhouettes in red
Against the arid dust of evening's sky,
And these sad words, the only record left
Of the meteor which blazed that night so long ago
To briefly light the desert's vast expanse.

Dreamscape

This is the setting of the recurrent dream,
A horizon edged by a turquoise sea,
The scrub-pines and royal palms of Jamaica
Fanning softly in a warm wind
The rhythmic shrieking of tree toads
In the undergrowth, and constant roar
Of homing waves, irrational,
Impatient as a longing lover.

This is the backdrop,
Overgrown, winding roads, volcanic hills
Thrust up in the violent long-ago.
Night after night, primal memories
Repeat, surging, pushing up layers
Of forgotten bedrock, obsession's quest
This dream-world. Departure time,
Yet hidden under heavy cloud
The sun of the tropics remains,
And unsuppressed, insistent the rhythm
Drums on, and with it unrest continues.

Now, into the interior, ascending hills,
Above, clouds of emerald parrots, flame-of-the-forest,
Green juxtaposed against orange,
Feverish, the dreamer climbs on, compelled,
Until she sees the old plantation walls,
Moldering, choked in philodendron,
The crumbling stones of its portals,
A last remnant of evil, the link
To the forsaken, whose children
One day would claim this hated land,
Measured in chains, for their own.

Long silent from these ruins, the slave chants
And whips' lash. Now this graveyard becomes
The nightly roaming-ground for her spirit,
Bound in other chains invisible and silent.

The Straw Woman

She has carried her woven baskets and dolls
From far up in the hills, down
To the straw market of Negril.
Over years, an unforgiving sun
Has etched a silver film
Onto her dark eyes, staring
From a wrinkled brown face.
She waits for someone to stop
And admire, perhaps to buy,
But this, and every day, her need
Must not appear too urgent: neutral and polite
She will wait, then at sunset,
Gather her goods together
For the trek up overgrown, green, winding paths
Back over the mud trace, a dotted line on the map.

So many days, I, too, have journeyed
From safe seclusion in the heart's hills,
Waiting for someone to stop and notice
My straw doll, with its brave, stitched-on smile,
Carried from childhood, carefully protected,
Waiting for that day when eyes
Would alight on it and be pleased.
Now a stranger enters the marketplace,
And I know at once. Nearing, he sees the doll,
Picks it up, cups it in his palm, holds it to his face,
Then as suddenly, he sets it down, turns away,
Eyes filled with regret, and leaves wordless,
In a moment, just a figure on the horizon.

Now the sun has burned the hillsides orange
And it slips swiftly into the sea, nightfall in the tropics.
And like the straw woman, I pack the worn doll
Back into my bag of dreams and longing
And withdraw into solitude's rugged landscape.

Vigil

From a white-washed cottage atop
A hillside of tangled vines and hibiscus
And orchards of wild limes, far below
The sea glinting aquamarine,
I watch in vigilant resignation
For a sighting, a sail to appear

Night after night, a bonfire lights the rocks
For his return. The dream resurfaces,
Restless rocking of a soul at sea.
Yet I wake back here, high in the hills, alone
To the sweet morning-song of birds
After the pelting of an early rain,
And now a sun which bursts, blinding,
Over the blue expanse.

Misbegotten

From afar she watches his comings and goings,
Navigating by that distant star,
Once brilliant and close,
As suddenly, shot meteor-like
Out of her orbit,
Its light now as hard to fix
As the seventh of the Seven Sisters,
Blinking as it travels
Over light years
Through stellar dust
To cast its faint image
Like his fleeting smile,
Onto her searching eyes,
The few warm words
Onto her straining ears,
Led to this fated place
As the thread of life unravels.

And on clouded nights,
Though not visible, the ghost
Of a star rises, re-invokes
The shine through shrouded heavens,
Which she once saw in his gaze,
In that one charmed hour.
Now, only from a distance, or by chance,
She encounters a glimpse of his face,
Stolen moments, quick intense phrases,
And in future time, in her mind she will trace
His whereabouts, the day all but forgotten,
Still guided by that ghostly star
Which once shone its luminous hope
On a love, beautiful, but misbegotten.

Awakening

The cello's somber notes, a reckoning,
Its deep and sonorous tones, a morning hymn,
Hanging like mist over the mountain range
White and low beyond the lake's blue limn,
Begs her at last to sing the heart's lament
Compels the oracle within to speak,
Intensified by violin and flute
Weaves a melancholy fantasy.

How slow and hard her naive daydreams die,
How steep the cost of leaving them behind.
A mountain range of clouds banks the sky,
Once blue, building to thunderheads:
It soon must come, the prophesy fulfilled,
The script in which all inwardly coheres
Left behind, anxiety and fear,
Sadness abandoned to the dusty past.

Instead we waken to a different script:
The fairy tale without a happy end.
Cellos and violins sing out their dirge
And as our soul's surrogate they weep.
Our journey sallies forth in fits and starts,
Brief, halcyon days, for nature benison
Will not be begged or wheedled or cajoled
And time blasts past us, age supplanting youth
Dismayed and ever farther from our goal,
At the rift between imagining and truth.
The world, chimera: only deep within
Are peace and joy and love vouched safe,
As transient as this August morning breeze
Fleeting as the wind-blown ripples on the lake.

Invocation and Benediction

Beyond the mist-carved lake and opposite shore
The vast green ridge of mountains sprawls,
Wrapped in dense clouds, clinging magnetic,
Drawn then held by heavy ore.
Down here, the sun lights the bending birch
Reflects the low-grown scrub, the clapboard hut,
Their images distortions in the ripples.
Borne on the wind, short, excited cries,
Gold-finches, calling over flinty sand
Blend with the cicada's choir:
Peace is mirrored in the lake's wavy glass,
Succor in the tumult of this life.

My thoughts return to him, so far from here
Who, like these mountains, shrouded in fog,
Fights to feel the sun, to see the light
No one can conjure up to shine,
Groping for that hidden rocky pass
Through the wilderness surrounding him.
As if in mime, my lips shape words
He cannot hear, nor is he warmed by an embrace,
Numb, the only comfort he receives,
The fragment of a greeting. As if palsied,
He sits unmoved, senses all distorted,
Perceiving threat where none is harbored,
Carefully I measure every word,
As talking through minefields, I try to honor
The line between abandonment and trust,
Weighing the need for space with that for warmth.

The screen behind closed eyes reveals no answer
But as I open them the scene restores.

The sight of lake and pine-cloaked hills,
The solitude of water washing sand,
Lapping rocky ledges in soft wind:

Let this stillness be my wellspring and my guide,
That as he searches for an untapped strength,
Watching powerless from the other shore,
This the hardest thing of all, I'll do,
Bear witness to his struggle, and abide.

Diagnosis

As the skillful surgeon lets infection draw,
Before incising the boil's heat with deft blade,
Releasing poisons long fomenting there,
Contaminating the afflicted body,
So, she takes up the pen to cut through paper,
Unleashing words to grasp the inchoate,
Trapped long ago inside, to now flood forth,
Its tide dammed up for years, in the hope
This unrelenting woe would someday cease,
No longer be a need to lend it voice,
That as the dolor and the calor ebbed,
The fever having raged and reached its crisis
Would then burn out, subside in soothing lysis
The patient wake, as if from fitful sleep,
Exhausted from the struggle, but now whole.
Just so she waited for that perfect time.

But life invokes a different metaphor,
Not weeks or months suffice to convalesce.
And only after years it all comes clear:
A malady from birth without a cure.
That never flagging will to make him whole
Concedes defeat as truth's unflinching eye
Stares her down, and humbled, she retreats.
The pen tears sheets in disbelief:
The story gone awry since its inception,
The script distorted, manuscript all twisted.
The malady was present in the womb,
Innocent, ensnared by helices corrupt.
Not early blight, the opposite in fact:
A child's illness present in the man,
Dormant through the years. What seemed

Incongruent now solves the mystery.
The puzzle comes together and coheres.
The pen dissects through strata of denial,
Cuts to the source, a silent place,
Where raw fear lives, so deep it cannot heal,
Except to granulate from inside out.
It cannot mend without a thickened scar,
Unlike a clean cut, neatly to be closed,
Bound up with gauze and tape, it must be left
Unsutured, open to the air.

She turns away from the Medusa's face.
Her questions, yet unanswered, circle back
To touch upon the critical dilemma.
Will she be doomed to live beyond his days?
Outlive her child, unnatural, this end.
Or he remain alone upon this earth
Vulnerable, unable to defend,
Comfortless as she must journey on?
A bleak expanse, beyond the dark abyss,
An unplumbed reservoir of salty tears,
Which threatens to engulf a mother's heart,
And both are left to cling to bare rock-face.

And yet this coast might be a better fate
Than left adrift at sea, no shore in view.
Though harsh, the sight of this uncharted land
Might well be better than the lot of those,
Remaining without answers untold years,
Unrecognized, left rudderless to roam.
Here, on the distant shore, beyond despair,
She has the sense at last of coming home.

Scarecrow

Fluttering in the chill breeze,
His tattered scarecrow figure stands
Lone, visible for miles
Left out on a sepia-tone plain,
Stripped of leafy comfort,
Like barren maples
On the opposite hill:
Hope's bower rent apart.
But unlike trees, whose dormancy
Dreams of a pale-green future time,
No such visions occupy
His storm-tossed, tortured brain,
Nor can he turn back to look upon
A past bathed in sunlit promise,
Back to behold a summer's radiance.
Planted in an ominous now
He senses only fall's chill specter
Grasping at his ever thinner body,
Threatening its meager substance,
Mocking his scarecrow's scowl.
The raucous crow's cry rings hollow,
Echoes back, sounding defeat,
And I am called to task
For asking him to stay,
To live in emptiness and pain.

But I do ask, make this request,
In the vain dream that someday
His straw stuffing will be replaced
By warm flesh, that a real heart
Will beat again in his forsaken chest,
That a dawning sun will light that dim cave

Where his mind's held hostage.
And in the hope that Spring
Will one day take him by surprise,
Tear him from winter's withering grip,
And bring him back to walk again with us.

Fortune Teller

There was a time she would have sought a seer,
Extended, innocent, her outstretched palm,
Asked that the Tarot cards be shuffled, read
Approached the gypsy lacking any fear:
Those were her charmed and halcyon years,
Each dawn unfolding water lily-like,
Each evening blessed by song of mockingbirds.
She would have met Cassandra unabashed,
Inwardly secure, her soul assured
Whatever iterations came to light,
Through second sight (though yet undreamt)
Must be benign or even bring delight:
These being merely variations,
Renditions of the harmony of life.

Yet should the tea leaves' trace, in fact, bode ill:
Of random tragedy or dreams disturbed,
This she'd ascribe to idle superstition
Continue on her path quite unperturbed,
Ignore, if something presaged a collision
Convinced that nothing untoward could supervene,
To alter or deter her fate's direction.

But dense clouds came to chase away clear skies,
Which stretched before her eyes just yesterday.
Now storm banks drape the sun, no light escapes
And leaden skies alone predominate.
Would it have helped to know what was to come,
Could good result, if knowing couldn't change?
Now after years, again the sun breaks through
A few bright rays slant downward to her vale,

The question of tomorrow or next year
She chooses not to query, leaves instead
In the realm of the unasked and the unanswered,
There at the fork of hope and unwept tears.

The Craftsman's Grief

The finely-tuned grand piano stands
Exquisitely crafted in the still,
Draped room, untouched.
In dreams, the cabinetmaker perceived
Chords of Beethoven and Brahms
Ringing from its keys, those sounds
To captivate all in their magic reach,
Each wire twisted, ivory keys hand-hewn,
Then padded with purple coat of felt,
Placed with care beneath each hammer:
The spring investing white and black perfection.
A masterpiece imbued with timeless craft,
The piano-maker's secrets. At last
The polished instrument
Stands here alone, untouched,
In this airless room, where drapes
Obscure locked windows, guard against
A single beam of stray sunlight
Or mere stirring of a fresh breeze.
The prodigy for whom this piece was made,
Lives in a nightmare and he cannot wake.

And so the perfect grand stands undisturbed
Sleeps its own untouched virgin sleep.
And for all the skill of his creation
The craftsman grieves for melodies
That never will be heard, for the sad truth
That he cannot cause a single note
To issue forth or be distilled
From the ivory of this keyboard:
His grief is that of nascent promise
Which will lie fallow, never be fulfilled.

Samsara

The rounded mountain range crouches
In deepest fog this rainy dawn.
The knowledge of its winding paths and streams,
Impenetrable, obscured by clouds and mist,
Material of mystery and dreams.
One foreground ridge stands out in crystal view,
As rain, staccato, pocks the slate-grey lake,
A string of clouds stretches at its edge,
A blurred reflection in the charcoal pond.

She sits here seeking mooring,
Demands of heaven, where the sun has fled,
Beseeches of the rain-cloaked hills,
Must darkness be his metaphoric world,
In time will answers be forthcoming,
If so, might they then signal change,
Improve the outcome in this high-stakes game?

And though she never meant to cause him harm,
Still unavoidable, this wrenching guilt.
Mordant taste of unaccomplished dreams
Without fulfillment, bitter drink, this truth.
Briefly, she can forget the leaden weight,
Drop worry, let it levitate away,
And she has learned to live within a world,
Where beautiful and cruel coexist,
To celebrate these mountains, flinty beach,
Aware of summer's brief domain,
And found acceptance of life's random flow.

Yet still so much eludes her reach,
To cast aside the steel-trap in her breast,

And spend whatever days remain carefree,
To search for, find the words which might console,
To leave behind the all-pervading grief,
Which clings like dense fog, to her soul,
Bear witness to his long-enduring pain,
And yet not bear it as her own.

Card Game

The bargaining chip, its edges worn from use
Has been cast upon the table.
His clear, blue eyes try to fix mine,
Which are brown, like a desperate player
Unable to resist any machination
To wear the dealer down.
First denying the bad hand,
Then, in time, accepting what's been dealt.
Exhausting every strategy, then, failing,
Left to grope through conversation
For some reason or answer.

It is I who pronounce sentence,
Speak the words of doom,
Break the guarded silence between us
With truth, eyes downcast, gently
Describing cells "gone awry,"
Unable to look him in the eye
And in that moment strangle hope
With the choking word "cancer."
Swallowing hard he understands "growth."

"Soften the blow. Give the poison in dilutions,"
The inner voice speaks, "in aliquots of truth,
Nothing in the Hippocratic Oath
Forbids circumlocution."
And then, a certain relief descends.
They all know the flesh is fragile,
That someday the end will come
And yet, before it had no form.
It might have happened in the Second War in France,
Or on a wet highway in a winter's storm

Returning from a New Year's party,
Or on a flight to some destination.
Now they know its shape just not the time.

And so, she bargains, his partner in crime,
Might they travel to the shore in September,
If he's not ill. I nod and deal the cards,
One by one, in this endgame of stalling,
All the while trying to remember
Not to build their house of cards too high.
Now they query how much time remains,
Once more ask the unanswerable,
And I fan the pack, spin the wheel,
Deal again, searching for the ace of hearts,
Knowing well the deck is stacked with spades.

Not weeks remaining, days. They ask how long.
Now looking full into their eyes I reply,
There is no definite time, and in their fashion,
They seem grateful for this uncertain scope
For that which no one can divine, for this collusion
Of their dealer in compassion, dealer in hope.

For Anne

In the early morning hours, the vision of a woman
Enters this quiet room, of slight shape
With pale blue eyes and reedy voice,
She speaks of grief, as she did yesterday.
But though I try, there is a lapse
Between us a chasm gapes
My words of comfort ring weak,
I reach out but cannot grasp
The loss of a child.

Lost, the shared journey of years.
It seems just last year the sweet baby clung
Then a few months since a small child ventured out
To hurry back to safe arms,
Now, without warning
Came the leap into the world
This all suddenly, finally erased
And a cloudless sky
Mirrors a mother's empty stare.

As she sits before me, there is no telling
What will survive or is gone without a trace.
Her heart is strong, with no beat missed,
And there is bell-like clarity of breath sounds.
Now, she turns with questioning face
And I search my heart for the parallel
Which does not exist, and words
Defer to a numb embrace. The easy lie,
That I understand her sunless days
Catches in my throat, left in the limbo of the unspoken.
As she leaves, my offering seems such a pale token.

Time and the day have passed, chill night half through,
Cold rain drumming at the window glass,
Inside this warm old house I rest,
Close the familiar sounds of children
Lost in dreams of days to come,
Their carefree laughter in play given over
To the soft, slow breathing of sleep.
At once, out of the darkness she appears.
A wave surges, rolling over, then
With its ebb, sucking me back
Into the deep well of my own fear
There lies the abyss.

Holding my breath, I rise
Move with urgency into the next room
Yet there my children lie, unharmed.
Standing on this threshold it comes clear.
Dear God! Let me never know the world
Of hollow eyes and empty arms.
Blind me to the revelations of that black land,
Devoid of hope. Some truths are best not learned.
But here in the dark room, the vision waits
And I cannot turn away.
Once more I reach out across the isolating space,
Covering my eyes, like Lot, to grope for
Then touch her outstretched hand.

Missing in Action

The photographs, like soldiers on her desk
In orderly chronology aligned,
His birth, then christening, confirmation,
The high school graduation,
Before long, his commission.
The faded picture postcard from Tikrit,
Displayed the message from his mission:
"Dear Mom and Dad, we've got them on the run!
Remember to collect my salary.
I'm fine. I love you. Your son, John."
And that concludes the little gallery.

One telling photo missing from the group,
For only with it gone can she regress,
Dwell on his handsome smiling face:
Private First Class Johnny, in full dress,
This portrait always given pride of place.
The source of all her tears has long gone dry,
But far-off looks and sighs give her away,
Trust drowned by the constant echo: Why?
Sent in to locate "weapons of destruction"
Never questioning the authorized portrayal.
No lofty goal, just avarice for oil,
And he fell prey to war's seduction,
Caught in the steel trap of its betrayal.

How distant now, the show of pomp and glitter,
The call-to-arms, a righteous, urgent cause.
Deceit, exposed, now cuts her to the core.
The photo of a young man's flag-draped box,
Lies face-down in a dusty bureau drawer.

Lullaby for a Soldier in Fallujah

Recall how eighteen years ago he laughed
Unselfconscious, cradled in adoring arms.
How you caressed the silken baby skin,
Later ran in his reckless, toddling wake
To catch his missteps, break his frequent falls,
Comfort his cuts and bruises with adhesive patches.
Remember how you strove to keep him safe,
Electric outlets covered, poisons under lock,
A sturdy gate to guard him from the stairs:
Precautions to protect his fledgling life.

Now, far from your once watchful eyes,
Turning from one sand hill to another,
Warily, he sniffs the desert air,
Which suddenly might blow caustic,
Burning, blistering or worse yet blinding.
He waits alone, far from your protection.

Call back to mind the nights you paced the floor,
Whose boards creaked testimony to each tooth,
Cutting through tender gums, the fairy
Wedging silver coins beneath his pillow,
The cutting, later on the loss of teeth,
The ministrations of a kindly dentist.

Before he left, a different check performed:
A detailed catalog of every tooth
In case someday only his fillings
Could sort out his remains from bits of rubble.

Remember teaching him to search for beauty,
Learn the names of flowers, birds and trees,

How you reviewed his school work nightly,
Taught him by example to respect and love.
Those eighteen years spent in careful rearing
Now seem like dust scattered to the winds.

One night a fever raged and he convulsed.
You ran, carrying him to his doctor's door:
Elixirs given at set times,
Patiently you sponged his small hot form,
Held vigil by his wicker bassinet
Until the crisis passed at dawn,
The fever spent, the croup now stilled
And he lay pale in his tent of mist.
Each month his weight plotted on a graph,
Measured, recorded in a treasured tome,
Chronicle of birth and milestones.

Then other measurements were made:
For army boots and combat uniform:
To soon be measured in machine gun's site,
Measured for the box to bear him home.
Recall the day he fell in love, and you,
Sat by helpless as his young heart broke.
Watched as time healed and he reached out again,
This time successful, love requited,
Witnessed a wrenching parting from his love
At the airbase when his recent call-up came.

Now in this desert place, prepared and armed,
Though he has learned the war-games well enough,
Rehearsed the tactics, well-designed maneuvers,
Mastered all the strategy and moves,
This chess board now appears so unfamiliar.
He scans with rapid breath and pounding heart.

In combat dress, adroit in all commands.
How can he ever execute this part,
Raised as he was to love and not to kill?
He pushes forward, body in slow motion
Into the blasting chaos, burning sand,
To screams and shouts, and sees no semblance
To those routines he practiced at the base,
And yet this is what the drills were all about:
No more straw dummies tossed into the air,
Like driven chaff, now human beings fly,
Skyward then mutilated back to earth,
And at his side their eyes roll upward,
The final glimpse, a flawless azure dome.

Some months ago, in quiet time alone,
You spoke to him of giving and of trust,
In lack of certainty, of keeping faith:
What bearing does that have on this equation?
Under the winking desert stars he waits
Praying for rain to rinse away the dust
But the drenching comfort never comes,
Instead just horror, the raining of shells
As missiles scream war's wanton lullaby.
What good was all your tender care till now?
Grenades and bombs rock him to fitful sleep,
He dreams of life meticulously planned
Of hopes all mothers harbor in their souls
But never have the power to fulfill,
Promises that life will never keep.

Sint Maarten

When it has reached full ripeness, not before
That poem will begin to write itself,
Already formed, flow freely from the pen,
Having burned within for far too long
Will weep, at last, those private, pent-up tears
Will sort through all those grains of sand,
Which poured in tedious rhythm
For five years through this hourglass,
Sift for meaning, even sift for truth
Search for reason, for some hidden light,
To cull from bleak days of the past,
In retrospect, attempt to theorize,
Try to reveal some hidden sense
Buried in the miasma of the chaos,
Which long besieged her being,
Days which drifted into weeks, then years,
The heat of deepest passion, swallowed up,
Lost, that one last chance for joy,
Swept in the rushing river out to sea
The residue left in silt, compassion
For those who journey on through darkness.
No. It will not be coaxed or forced, that poem,
But in time's passing, it will write itself.

Out of the Silence

For Herbert Morris   August 1997

Alone this morning by a glassy sea,
Above a heavy blanket of gray cloud.
One upon the next, waves curl in to beach
Thrown up from the forgotten ocean floor
To crest then crash upon the sandy verge,
Carry with them voices from the distant past
Summoned from the depths of sudden grief.
Their images march in senseless file
Call out across the panoramic sweep,
Ripped from the weave of this world,
Leaving a gaping rent in time's tapestry.
Histories disparate, chaotic as breakers
Building here, then there to roll away
Spreading to east then west, sliding back,
To wash into the ebbing slate of sea,
Lives nascent, vanished without notice
At once their roles written from life's script,
Unveiling there a yawning, random void.

Mirrored in the littoral's crushed shells
The reflection of Russell's shining face,
Beloved at school, champion of games,
Dragged down in a fever's undertow,
His vigor wasted in a few short weeks:
An apple tree now blooms where once he played

The wind picks up, shaking the stiff dune grass,
Another vision floats upon damp air,
Commencement's ceremony just concluded,
Skimming an outboard's rocky wake,
A boat reversed, a boy caught by the blade,

A mortal wound, no help in reach
And Peter's blood ebbed into the bay's blue wash.

The waves crash in, slapping the jetty stones
As glaucous seagulls keen and hover,
Their mewling calls resemble human cries.
Unswerving, memory's tape rewinds,
The mind moves backward to that bleakest place
Where the flotsam of those taken early drifts.

From the deepest void Beth's voice resounds,
The flowers at the chapel altar fresh,
The bridal couple on their wedding trip
Their uneventful flight at once cut short
The plane drawn magnetically to mountaintop,
Pitching in flames onto volcanic rock,
The evening news reports no one survives.

The ocean roars, pounds the wooden pilings,
Above the din, lifting on the breeze,
Voices call, unresolved in their leaving.
Blank whiteness, as car collides with tree,
Snow-mobile against a snowplow's steel.
Black memories mix with the plover's cry:
Events exempt from all interrogation,
Sentenced without trial, without hearing,
No judge or jury sitting in attendance
To summon someone, something to account.

As green foam crests beneath the fog-bound limn,
My thoughts return to you, my grieving one.
A young friend wrested from your side,
Her spirit cognizant of light but too of darkness,
At once snuffed out, her car met head-on
By speeding truck on a busy highway,

The world deprived of her poetic vision.
And you are left to sort through fractured truth,
Sift shards of sense from meaningless detritus.

Where are the rituals or soothing rites
To promise us the hope of a reunion
Upon some gleaming future shore? The sea
In randomness drifts back to its depths.
No answer washes up upon the sand,
And all along this lonely sweep of beach.
No comfort for those voices from the void
No resolution, just the surf's white noise,
No redress, for their sudden disappearance
And laughter drowned in the ocean's wild roar.
No solace for those left behind, abandoned,
Standing numbly by the windswept coast,
To stare at the chaotic vastness.

What source might furnish strength, compassion?
What tourniquet applied could staunch the loss,
And who articulate the pain, or sing
The painful dirge of those departed young?
Who paint the canvas of hope and healing,
Build the retaining wall of words
Against the onslaught of this crashing surf?
Who hold the shield to that Medusa's face?
Only the poet, who in sorrow's vise
Must cast his net for those swept overboard,
Must set a line despite the raging seas,
Seine for those souls, reclaim them from the deep
Wrest them from the undertow of grief
Give voice to their abruptly silenced song,
Retrieve the good of lives brief but well-lived,
To find within our hearts their final rest.

Stork Song
Gunsbach, Alsace, 1990

High above rounded old mountains,
Brushed in wildflower pastels,
May's earthy breath on the breeze,
He soars and glides
Between wisps of cloud and blue,
Looking down on terra cotta village roofs,
In the foothills of the Vosges.
He dips and rides on this afternoon sky,
Gentle stork, bringer of good fortune,
Long legs trailing out behind
Like a kite-tail.

And we, earthbound, fill with awe
At this free, unselfconscious being,
As he drops and soars, dips and glides,
Our spirits rise to meet his
For an airy moment,
Then plunge back to earth
Once more subject to gravity's thrall.

Mnemonic for Kezar Lake

The low white mountains lie in smoky haze,
Backdrop to a pine and birch-clad stage
By the gentle lapping water, Kezar Lake
Upon whose surface sailboats, kayaks skim
The undulating wake, disturbed by wind
And intermittent motor launch,
Slaps the grainy sand and then recedes,
A pendulum of summer. To return,
These careworn feet have covered miles
To reach this time warp, far removed retreat,
Drawn by chords of Chopin and of Brahms
Resounding, this morning, by the lake
Which glistens like the facets of a gem.

Listening from this sheltered cove,
Draped in deep green clinging moss
Snug in scrub, lined by granite rock
Encrusted in lichen's malachite,
Sentinels which line the rounded bank,
All silent now but for the goldfinch call,
Cicadas' drone, the quavering of loons,
This is my lookout on a water-world
Alien to worry and commotion
A canvas struck of lake, clouds and hills,
Devoid of civilized confusion.
A female mallard, called as if on cue,
Drifts in to shore and blinks a shiny eye,
Calls into question all the rush and hurry,
How much is real or merely an illusion
In this brief life: she slowly fans her tail
And as she floated in, so she sets sail.

And I, relieved for now from daily drudge,
Granted space and time to intervene
Enter this calm zone, released from stress,
Exempt from care and out of heartache's reach.
And months from now, returning in my dreams,
The vision of this place will be with me
Of harmony and nature's solitude,
Preserved in memory as perfect peace.

Variably Cloudy
Roaring Branch, November 1999

Bulrushes, tall water reeds bow,
Rustle in the stirring morning air
In waving ripples the sun's bright disk
Reflects despite dense clouds
Moving across, obscuring
Then again and again it shines through
Warming, affirming summer's primacy.

Surfacing fish blow concentric rings
Which spread, blend with the pond's
Wind-whipped crosshatch pattern
This singular complex microcosm
Fluid, ever-changing yet constant.

A crow sounds piercing warning calls
Perhaps possessed of second sight,
Aware of things as yet not manifest,
Of a vague chill on the rising wind
Whispering overhead, blowing
Over the countryside, spread out
Before her, over round hay bales
Copse of birch and buttonwood
Dotting the browning hillsides.
Cicadas' shrill resounds insistently
Though less frenetic. These subtler signs
She'd ardently deny, refuse to read,
The prophesy of winter's nearing hush,
To revel in November's lingering,
Decide a while longer just to dally
Beside this pond, beside the waving rush
In the stillness of an Indian summer valley.

Garden of Eden
Quisisana, August 1993

A stand of pines reflects in waving water,
The only sound cicadas, chickadees,
The humming motor on the lake,
And loons, who whistled through the night,
With dawn's arrival drifting into sleep.

Her senses close upon this peaceful still
But not to shut it out, to lock it in.
Each inhaled breath exhaled in slower rhythm
Withdrawing from her mind those darker thoughts
Gently to release their hold, drop them away.
A hidden door is open to white light,
Pure energy, not dream, or plan or thought:
Now merging with a wider world of light,
Devoid of fear and hope but yet aware.

A feeling close now, almost within reach,
Preconscious joy, beyond the scope of words:
This must be how it was so long ago,
Viewed at the world's morn, that pristine garden
Where suddenly the sentient mind awoke
And yet before the yoke of thought was born.

Autumn Sonata

Overnight, heaps of brittle leaves
Have obscured the lawn,
Blown down one autumn evening
From the silver maple, which swayed
Just yesterday in August's wind.
Now bare twigs and branches thrust
Stiffly at the chill dark night,
All foliage shed, fossils of summer's shade,
Just as sighs and mute glances,
Fall from hearts, remnants of love's
Full leaf, and empty arms are lifted
Like branches toward a gray sky.

Acknowledgments

My heartfelt thanks goes to my loving family for their support, as well as to friends for tolerating my periodic need for solitude. A very special place needs mention: Quisisana, in Maine, birthplace of many of these poems. I am grateful to Jane and Sam Orans for providing this beautiful oasis. I want to express my appreciation to my sister, Katherine Plotnicov, for her assistance in helping to edit the manuscript and for her photography.

I want to thank my lifelong friend, Robert Temple, writer and poet, for his great help and encouragement. He is author of a dozen books. He translated Rilke's *Sonnets to Orpheus,* and the *Epic of Gilagmesh,* in verse, which was performed at the Royal National Theatre in London.

CPSIA information can be obtained at www.ICGtesting.com
Printed in the USA
BVOW07s1329060913

330351BV00002B/21/P